# WORLD STUDIES

# SOUTH AMERICA

by Michael Regan

**FOCUS READERS.**

V@YAGER

# www.focusreaders.com

Focus Readers is distributed by North Star Editions:
sales@northstareditions.com | 888-417-0195

Produced for Focus Readers by Red Line Editorial.

Content Consultant: Paola Canova, PhD, Assistant Professor of Anthropology and Teresa Lozano Long Institute of Latin American Studies, University of Texas at Austin

Photographs ©: Shutterstock Images, cover, 1, 4–5, 7, 8–9, 11, 14–15, 17, 23, 25, 27, 28–29, 32, 34–35, 40–41, 43, 44; AP Images, 13; iStockphoto, 19, 20–21; Taylor Weidman/LightRocket/Getty Images, 31; Leo Correa/AP Images, 37; David Mercado/Reuters/Newscom, 39

**Library of Congress Cataloging-in-Publication Data**
Names: Regan, Michael, 1946- author.
Title: South America / Michael Regan.
Description: Lake Elmo, MN: Focus Readers, 2021. | Series: World studies |
    Includes index. | Audience: Grades 7-9
Identifiers: LCCN 2020003418 (print) | LCCN 2020003419 (ebook) | ISBN
    9781644934036 (hardcover) | ISBN 9781644934791 (paperback) | ISBN
    9781644936313 (pdf) | ISBN 9781644935552 (ebook)
Subjects: LCSH: South America--Juvenile literature.
Classification: LCC F2208.5 .R44 2021  (print) | LCC F2208.5  (ebook) | DDC
    980--dc23
LC record available at https://lccn.loc.gov/2020003418
LC ebook record available at https://lccn.loc.gov/2020003419

Printed in the United States of America
Mankato, MN
012021

# ABOUT THE AUTHOR

Michael Regan worked as a community college and university career counselor before turning his attention to research and writing. He is especially interested in topics related to technology and current events. In his spare time, he enjoys watercolor painting, hiking, tai chi, and reading. He lives in southern Arizona with his spouse and two cats.

# TABLE OF CONTENTS

# CHAPTER 1

# WELCOME TO SOUTH AMERICA

South America stretches from just north of the equator to far south near Antarctica. Rainforests, mountains, massive cities, and small villages make up this continent. South America is the fourth-largest continent on Earth. More than 425 million people live there. Approximately half of those people live in Brazil. This country is the largest in South America. More than 20 million people live in Brazil's largest city, São Paulo.

**Thick jungles cover many of Colombia's mountains.**

Guyana, Suriname, and French Guiana lie to the north of Brazil. French Guiana is a territory of France. It is not independent. Venezuela and Colombia are in the northwestern part of South America. Colombia is the continent's second-largest country by population. Its capital, Bogotá, is located in the Andes Mountains.

Ecuador, Peru, and Chile cover the rest of the Pacific coast. Cuzco, Peru, is one of the oldest cities in the Americas. It was also the capital of the Inca Empire. Bolivia and Paraguay are in the middle of the continent. Most people in Paraguay speak Guaraní in addition to Spanish. Paraguay is the only country in the Americas where most people speak the same **Indigenous** language.

Argentina and Uruguay lie on the continent's southeastern coast. Buenos Aires, the capital of Argentina, is South America's second-largest city.

It is a center of business, culture, and the arts. Like South America as a whole, the city is full of incredible diversity.

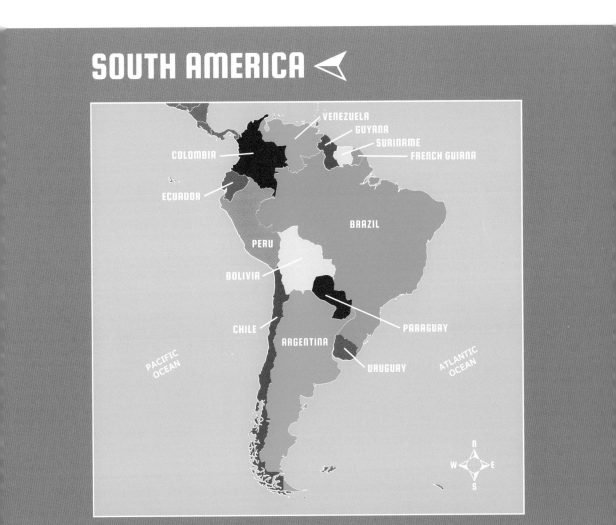

SOUTH AMERICA

VENEZUELA
GUYANA
SURINAME
COLOMBIA
FRENCH GUIANA
ECUADOR
BRAZIL
PERU
BOLIVIA
PARAGUAY
CHILE
ARGENTINA
URUGUAY
PACIFIC OCEAN
ATLANTIC OCEAN

# CHAPTER 2

# HISTORY OF SOUTH AMERICA

Humans have lived in South America for more than 14,000 years. For thousands of years, people moved around as they looked for food. Over time, however, groups of people started farming. When that happened, they began to settle. For example, the Las Vegas culture formed approximately 10,000 years ago. These people settled in present-day Ecuador. They grew several kinds of root vegetables and lived in small huts.

**The Norte Chico people of Peru built Caral. It is the oldest city in the Americas.**

By 3500 BCE, the Valdivia culture also developed in Ecuador. These people created early pottery.

In Peru, the Norte Chico people built large pyramids. They also developed systems to water crops. Their **civilization** lasted from approximately 3000 to 1800 BCE.

The region's first empires began developing in the 400s CE. The Tiwanaku Empire formed in Bolivia. Its main city was home to tens of thousands of people. In the 1300s, the Chimú Empire formed in Peru. However, the Inca Empire defeated the Chimú in 1470. In the early 1500s, the Inca Empire was the largest nation on Earth. During this time, tens of millions of Indigenous people lived in South America.

The continent experienced huge changes in the 1500s. European colonists came to South America. The Spanish defeated the Inca. Portugal,

France, and the Netherlands also took control over parts of the region. Europeans enslaved Indigenous peoples. But many groups resisted Europeans. For example, the Mapuche people fought off the Spanish for hundreds of years.

## THE INCA EMPIRE, 1527 ◁

PACIFIC OCEAN

ATLANTIC OCEAN

◼ INCA TERRITORY

N
W E
S

Even so, Europeans brought diseases with them. Indigenous people had never been exposed to these diseases. Millions died as a result.

Colonists wanted new workers. So, they enslaved millions of people in Africa. They sent the enslaved Africans to South America and forced them to work on plantations. Enslaved Africans faced brutal and violent conditions.

By the mid-1600s, Spain and Portugal controlled most of the region. But in the 1800s, South American colonists pushed for independence. Spain's colonies broke into nine countries. They included Colombia, Venezuela, and Argentina. Portugal's colony formed only one country, Brazil. Border disputes erupted among the countries. Argentina, Brazil, and Uruguay won a war against Paraguay. Chile won a war against Bolivia and Peru.

In 1983, people in Argentina voted for the first time since a dictatorship took power in 1976.

In the 1900s, the United States started to influence the region. During this time, most South American governments swung between democracies and **dictatorships**. The United States helped topple several democratic governments. It also supported several military dictatorships. It did so for political and economic reasons.

During this period, Guyana and Suriname gained independence. Democracies returned over time. But many peoples, especially Indigenous peoples, still struggled for rights and freedoms.

# GEOGRAPHY AND CLIMATE

Large bodies of water surround South America. The Atlantic Ocean borders the east and north. The Caribbean Sea lies along the northwestern coast. And the Pacific Ocean borders South America's western coast.

The Andes Mountains run along the entire Pacific coast. The Andes are the longest mountain system on Earth. Their tallest mountain is called Aconcagua. This mountain is in Argentina.

**The Andes Mountains stretch for more than 4,300 miles (7,000 km).**

South America is home to three large river basins. A river basin is an area of land that drains rain and snow into the same river. The Amazon basin is the largest in the world. It covers most of northern South America.

North of the Amazon is the Orinoco basin. The Orinoco flows through Brazil, Colombia, and much of Venezuela. This region is mostly grassland. Those grasslands are called the llanos.

The Paraguay-Paraná basin is in the southeast of the continent. The basin provides water to the most important farming and ranching areas of South America. This fertile area is called the Pampas.

Plains cover parts of Brazil's, Chile's, and Peru's coasts. These low-lying lands feature dry climates. For example, the Atacama Desert is in Chile. It is the driest non-polar desert on

Guanacos graze in the Pampas of northern Argentina.

Earth. Some parts have received no rain at all in known history.

In contrast, the nearby Andes can receive large amounts of snow. The weather there also tends to be cool. Meanwhile, much of northern South America is tropical. These areas, such as the Amazon, receive large amounts of rain. They are also humid. At the same time, the region's southern tip features a much colder climate. For this reason, glaciers can be found there.

# THE AMAZON BASIN

The Amazon basin contains the largest tropical forest in the world. This forest covers an area approximately the size of the lower 48 United States. Most of the Amazon lies in Brazil. But it covers parts of eight other countries. Some of these include Peru, Colombia, Bolivia, and Venezuela.

The Amazon is home to 15 percent of the world's fresh water. It holds 10 percent of the world's **biodiversity**. Four hundred Indigenous groups live there as well. In addition, the Amazon is important for all life on Earth. Its trees and plants take in and store huge amounts of carbon dioxide ($CO_2$). High levels of this gas are a major cause of **climate change**. By taking in $CO_2$, the Amazon helps control this crisis.

However, the Amazon basin is in danger. One main reason is deforestation. This happens

▲ The Amazon rainforest is thought to contain approximately 16,000 species of trees.

when people clear large areas of a forest. More than 20 percent of the Amazon has already been cleared. Cattle ranching is the biggest cause of this problem. Farming, logging, mining, and wildfires are also causes. When forests are destroyed, they no longer absorb $CO_2$. They also release $CO_2$ into the air. As a result, destroying the Amazon makes climate change worse.

For many years, Brazil had reduced how much of the Amazon was being cleared. Between 2015 and 2020, however, deforestation increased again. Many experts worried that by 2040, it might no longer be possible to protect the Amazon.

# CHAPTER 4

# PLANTS AND ANIMALS

South America is home to a huge amount of biodiversity. Brazil, Colombia, Peru, and Venezuela are especially diverse. Each of those countries has at least 5,000 plant species that grow nowhere else in the world.

Approximately 80,000 plant species grow in the Amazon alone. Just 1 acre (0.4 ha) of land can have 100 kinds of trees. Some include silk cotton trees, Brazil nut trees, and rubber trees.

**The Quindío wax palm can only be found in Peru and Colombia. It is the world's tallest palm tree.**

The tops of these trees form a thick layer of leaves. Smaller plants such as ferns and orchids grow in the shade underneath. Long vines called lianas hang from trees like thick ropes.

Plants vary by the habitat where they grow. For example, the highland parts of the Andes are often cold. Most plants there are small. The plants' leaves tend to be stiff and strong. These features protect plants from freezing. One large plant is known as the Queen of the Andes. It grows in the mountains of Bolivia and Peru. This plant is the world's largest herb. The Queen of the Andes only flowers after it is at least 80 years old.

South America also features vast plains. These areas receive far less rain than rainforests. In northern South America, the llanos are mainly grassland. But coastal plains can be drier. Even fungus struggles to grow in the Atacama Desert.

△ Queen of the Andes plants can grow to be 50 feet (15 m) tall.

The continent's wide range of habitats also allows for much animal diversity. South America's river basins are home to millions of species. More than two million insect species live in the Amazon basin. Many insects and spiders are found nowhere else in the world. One of these spiders is the Goliath bird-eating tarantula. It is the largest tarantula on Earth. It eats insects, frogs, lizards, and even birds.

Hundreds of kinds of mammals also live in rainforests. These include primates, such as howler monkeys and spider monkeys. Sloths, otters, and tapirs live there, too. The capybara is the biggest rodent in the world. With all that prey, there must be predators. Two of the most fearsome are the jaguar and black caiman. The electric eel, anaconda, and boa are also deadly.

South America has thousands of species of freshwater fish. Piranhas, electric eels, and catfish are just a few. The continent also has approximately 3,000 species of birds. Some jungle birds are brightly colored, such as toucans

> ## ➤ THINK ABOUT IT

Do any of the plants and animals found in South America exist where you live? Why or why not?

▲ Capybaras can weigh more than 150 pounds (70 kg). They are larger than most dogs.

and macaws. Penguins, cormorants, and pelicans live along the coasts. The Andean condor soars over the Andes Mountains. It is one of the world's biggest flying birds.

South America's vast plains host a number of animals. Herds of llamas, alpacas, and vicuñas graze on grass and shrubs. These animals are related to camels. The plains are also home to foxes, guinea pigs, and deer. Everywhere on the continent is home to life-forms uniquely suited to their habitats.

# GREEN ANACONDAS

The green anaconda is the heaviest snake in the world. It can weigh up to 550 pounds (249 kg). This massive snake can be as long as a school bus. Its body can become 12 inches (30 cm) thick.

Green anacondas live in the Amazon and Orinoco basins. They tend to make their homes in swamps, marshes, and streams. These snakes are skilled swimmers. They spend much of their time in the water.

Once in the water, green anacondas can be hard to see. Only their eyes and nostrils stick above the surface. As a result, anacondas can breathe while mostly underwater. This ability allows them to hide as they wait for prey.

These snakes are constrictors. This means they squeeze their bodies around prey. The anaconda first squeezes until the prey's breathing and blood flow stop. Next, the snake's jaws open wide. Meals

Many green anacondas are more than 30 feet (9.1 m) long.

are eaten in one bite. Anacondas eat birds, pigs, and even jaguars. If a meal is big enough, the anaconda may not have to eat again for months.

Unlike many snakes, female anacondas do not lay eggs. They give birth to approximately 30 live snakes at one time. These babies are approximately 2 feet (61 cm) long. The babies swim and hunt as soon as they are born. In the wild, anacondas can live for 10 years. They can live for 30 years in zoos.

# CHAPTER 5

# NATURAL RESOURCES AND ECONOMY

South America has an incredible variety of natural resources. The geography of each country affects which resources it has. For example, lead and zinc are found at high elevations in the Andes Mountains. South America also has significant amounts of oil and gas. Venezuela is one of the largest oil producers in the world. In fact, oil makes up the majority of that country's **exports**.

**People have been collecting salt from salt mines in Maras, Peru, since ancient times.**

Metals are also important to the continent's economies. For instance, gold is a major export for Suriname and Guyana. South America holds 20 percent of the world's iron ore. This metal is often used to make steel. Brazil and Venezuela have especially large amounts of iron. In addition, Peru and Chile export nearly half of the world's raw copper.

Forests provide other important natural resources to the region. Chile exports plywood for building and wood pulp for making paper. At the same time, countries also depend on non-native trees, such as eucalyptus. This tree grows quickly. Companies manage eucalyptus plantations. People use the tree for construction throughout the continent.

In addition, many South American people rely on animal resources. A massive number of

△ The Indigenous Xikrin people of Brazil have used arrows to hunt fish in the Xingu River for centuries.

fish live in the Amazon's rivers. Many Indigenous peoples depend on these fish for food. Coastal countries also sell seafood to other countries.

Coffee beans start out red. They turn brown after being dried and roasted.

For instance, Peru and Chile sell a large number of anchovies. In Chile, there are also many salmon and trout farms. And much of Ecuador's economy depends on shrimp exports.

Agriculture is a major part of most South American economies. Brazil and Argentina are two of the world's largest producers of corn and soybeans. In fact, South America exports more than half of the world's soybeans. Farmers grow this crop throughout the Pampas region of Brazil and Argentina.

The climate of the Pampas supports cattle ranching as well. As a result, Brazil is one of the world's largest producers of beef. Cattle ranching also fuels the economies of Argentina, Paraguay, and Uruguay.

Other crops grow well in South America's tropical climates. Ecuador exports 25 percent of the world's bananas. Sugarcane and coffee are two of the continent's main tropical crops. Brazil is the world's largest seller of coffee. Colombia and Peru produce large amounts of coffee as well. Cacao is another major tropical crop. This bean is used to make chocolate.

## THINK ABOUT IT ◁

What natural resources exist where you live? What should people think about before using them?

# CHAPTER 6

# GOVERNMENT AND POLITICS

In every South American country, citizens elect their leaders. However, each country's government works differently. For example, Colombia's national government makes the main laws for its people. Argentina's national government makes many laws as well. But Argentina is made up of 23 provinces. These provinces also make major laws for the people who live there.

**The government of Argentina's Tucumán province meets in this building.**

In most South American countries, citizens vote for their president directly. But people tend to not select their lawmakers directly. Instead, they vote for political parties. Parties that win more votes receive more seats in Congress. But parties that win fewer votes still receive seats. As a result, countries often have many political parties.

Voting for parties instead of people can be helpful. For example, having many parties can give voices to many different perspectives. At the same time, many people in South America have problems with their political systems. These systems often deal with **corruption**. For this reason, few people in these countries feel represented by their lawmakers.

For example, Brazil elected an extremely **conservative** president in 2018. Between 2003 and 2016, a **socialist** party led the country. But

Brazilian citizens cast their votes during the 2018 presidential election.

corruption was common. Many people in Brazil did not agree with the new president's positions. But they felt extreme change was necessary.

Across South America, people have struggled for better leaders. Nicolás Maduro was first elected president of Venezuela in 2013. Living conditions became worse under Maduro. He also may have rigged his 2018 reelection. In 2019, a rival politician tried to take power from Maduro.

A number of countries supported this effort, including the United States. Many Venezuelans did as well. But as of early 2020, Maduro remained in power.

In Bolivia, the country's military forced the president to give up power in 2019. Evo Morales had been the first Indigenous president in South America. Morales's socialist programs brought more than one million people out of poverty. Most of these people were Indigenous. But Morales also supported businesses that harmed Indigenous people. And many people believed he rigged his 2019 election. Thousands of Bolivian people protested. In November 2019, Morales resigned.

Huge protests broke out in Chile in 2019 as well. Chilean students led many of these protests. People wanted the government to address the country's inequality. At the same time, Chile's

▲ Bolivian president Evo Morales attends a conference about global responses to refugees in 2017.

government had been more stable than many other South American governments.

Uruguay's government is also known for being stable. And between 2005 and 2019, Uruguay's government took many steps to improve its citizens' lives. For example, Uruguay began providing health care to all of its citizens. These changes had positive impacts on people across the country.

# CHAPTER 7

# PEOPLE AND CULTURE

South America is home to many peoples and cultures. Hundreds of Indigenous groups live there. For instance, millions of Quechua people live in the highlands of Bolivia, Peru, and Ecuador. The Quechua language is the most-spoken Indigenous language in the Americas. The Quechua people have a rich culture, too. In Peru, some Quechua people practice the scissors dance. Two dancers compete for up to 10 hours.

**The Quechua people have been weaving beautiful fabric with bright colors for centuries.**

The Mapuche people are another large Indigenous group. They make up 9 percent of Chile's population. Some also live in Argentina. In fact, these countries' borders have divided the Mapuche nation since the late 1800s. The Mapuche began living on this land long before Chile and Argentina were formed. For this reason, many Mapuche people are working to regain their land rights. They want to govern themselves.

Tens of millions of people also have African ancestry. Most live in Brazil. In fact, Afro-Brazilians are the country's largest ethnic group. They have helped create some of Brazil's major cultural traditions, such as samba. This tradition's roots come from the dances of enslaved West African people. There are many kinds of samba. But one common practice is known as the samba de roda. Dancers form a

Mapuche people protest in Santiago, Chile, in 2019.

circle. They clap and sing. Then each takes a turn dancing in the center of the circle.

Across South America, many parts of people's lives and cultures are still shaped by colonial relations. People who are descended from European colonizers still have power in many ways. For example, Spanish is the main language in most South American countries. Meanwhile, Brazil's most-spoken language is Portuguese.

A street market in São Paulo, Brazil, sells Japanese food and crafts.

In addition, Catholicism is the main religion on the continent. European colonizers spread this religion across South America. Even so, millions of people combine African religions with Catholicism. Protestant faiths are also growing. They are especially popular in Chile, Guyana, French Guiana, and parts of Brazil. There are also Jewish communities in South America. Most are in major cities. Religion's importance in people's lives also varies. In Uruguay, for example, religion is not important to most people.

There are also millions of people from more recent immigrant groups. People from around the world began to settle in South America in the early 1800s. A large number came from European countries, such as Italy. But many came from the Middle East and Asia as well. Tens of thousands of Lebanese people live in Ecuador. Approximately 40 percent of people in Guyana have Indian roots. And many people with Japanese backgrounds live in the region. In fact, South America is home to the highest number of Japanese people outside of Japan. South America's peoples are incredibly diverse and always changing.

## THINK ABOUT IT ◁

South America is diverse in many ways. What are some ways the area you live in is diverse?

# FOCUS ON
# SOUTH AMERICA

*Write your answers on a separate piece of paper.*

**1.** Write a paragraph describing the main ideas of Chapter 7.

**2.** Indigenous peoples continue to struggle for their lands and rights in South America. How do you think a country should respond to these kinds of demands?

**3.** What is the most-spoken Indigenous language in the Americas?

    **A.** Guaraní
    **B.** Spanish
    **C.** Quechua

**4.** Why is the Mapuche nation's land split between Chile and Argentina?

    **A.** Chile and Argentina were formed by taking over the Mapuche nation's land.
    **B.** The Mapuche nation invaded both Chile and Argentina.
    **C.** Chile's formation caused a Mapuche civil war, which split the nation in two.

*Answer key on page 48.*

# GLOSSARY

**biodiversity**
The number of different species that live in an area.

**civilization**
A large group of people with a shared history and culture.

**climate change**
A human-caused global crisis involving long-term changes in Earth's temperature and weather patterns.

**conservative**
Supporting traditional views or values, often resisting changes.

**corruption**
Dishonest or illegal acts, especially by powerful people.

**dictatorships**
Forms of government in which one leader has absolute power.

**exports**
Goods sent to other countries for sale.

**Indigenous**
Native to a region, or belonging to ancestors who lived in a region before colonists arrived.

**socialist**
Supporting a political system in which the government provides for basic needs, and where workers control the economy.

# TO LEARN MORE

## BOOKS

Adamson, Thomas K. *Learning About South America*. Minneapolis: Lerner Publications, 2016.

Foley, Erin L., Leslie Jermyn, and Caitlyn Paley. *Ecuador*. New York: Cavendish Square, 2016.

Gagne, Tammy. *Rain Forest Ecosystems*. Minneapolis: Abdo Publishing, 2016.

## NOTE TO EDUCATORS

Visit **www.focusreaders.com** to find lesson plans, activities, links, and other resources related to this title.

# INDEX

**Answer Key: 1.** Answers will vary; **2.** Answers will vary; **3.** C; **4.** A